SHIBA INU

A Comprehensive Guide for the Shiba Inu Personality and How to Train your Clever Shiba

by Stephanie Strauss

Table of Contents

Introduction

If you are reading this book, chances are, at the very least, you're thinking of having a Shiba Inu as part of your life, if you don't have one already. Shiba Inus are some of the best looking and most properly proportioned dogs that can also survive in most environments. They are very loyal and quite intelligent. They are, however, not for the faint-hearted and if you are a first time dog owner, a Shiba Inu might very well rule your house before you know it. Just because they are very intelligent, doesn't mean you can train them easily. Even seasoned dog trainers will admit that Shiba Inus are quite a handful. They need a self-confident and strong-willed master. If you are able to completely tame your Shiba Inu, then you are either a very lucky owner of the most obedient Shiba Inu in the world or you are quite a skilled dog person.

So what is a Shiba Inu anyway? Well, from the name itself you can probably guess that it is an Asian dog and you would be right. Shiba Inus are from the Land of the Rising Sun (Japan) and were originally bred to hunt various prey such as fowl, wild boar, and even bears. Yes, on some occasions, even bears. They are middle sized dogs with a heck of an energy level and smarts to boot. The Japanese have a few words to describe the Shiba Inu: *kaani-i* (spirited boldness), *soboku* (alertness), and *ryosei* (good nature). All together, this makes the Shiba Inu an interesting and strong willed hunting companion as well as a great living companion.

Shiba Inus only weigh about 20 lbs. but don't let this fool you. They are very athletic and strong for their size. They have a calm, independent, and confident demeanor; and often look at their world as if they own it. They are not the most social of animals, primarily because of their hunting lineage. The Shiba Inu is also known to be quite possessive of its toys and territory, and they do sometimes have aggressive tendencies towards other dogs, especially if they are of the same sex as the other dog. They were not bred to be social, although a little socialization can address this tendency when it is done in the early parts of the dog's life. But even when you have a well socialized Shiba, it can still be a coin toss whether or not he/she will be aggressive towards other animals. Because of this, most dog trainers suggest that you keep your Shiba on a leash when walking him to ensure that he does not pick a fight with other dogs or run away to try and catch a squirrel or cat.

Shiba Inus also shed, although most of the time their shedding is minimal. However, there is what Shiba Inu owners call "blowing their coat," which is when heavy shedding of the undercoat occurs. This happens mostly twice a year, one of which is usually in the spring when the cold winter weather begins to subside. It is not a big deal to worry about, but it is important to know the Shiba does require a fair amount of brushing during these coat-blowing periods. If you plan to let your Shiba Inu off her leash in your yard, make sure that you have a well secured yard. Remember that they are quite the escape artists thanks to their high level of intelligence and exploratory nature. Obedience training is highly suggested in their early years to improve their temperament. Training can improve certain things but you cannot always expect them to come at your beck and call like a Golden Retriever.

Chapter 1: Background of the Shiba Inu

A Shiba Inu literally means "brushwood dog." It is the smallest of the hunting dogs that originated from Japan. It was originally bred to hunt alongside humans to take on larger prey like wild game, boars, and even bears. They are very agile and intelligent which makes them perfect for their primary purpose of hunting. The Shiba Inu has also been a part of the Japanese culture and is seen in many old Japanese pictures and drawings alongside another Japanese legend, the Samurai. Yes, they are hunting dogs but unlike Bloodhounds, Labradors, or even Golden Retrievers, they were not usually taken hunting along with other dogs. They are active hunters in a sense that they take an active part in the hunt and don't just retrieve dead game. As a hunter, all you need is a Shiba Inu and you're set.

Shiba Inus are sometimes mistaken for Akitas but there are a lot of differences between the two breeds. For one, the Akita is a lot larger than the Shiba Inu. They are easily identifiable with their proportionally small, triangular, and perky ears. The head is proportionally large, and their cute muzzle has a mild vertical forehead and then slightly tapers towards the nose. They have a double coat, a thick and soft undercoat and a straight and stiff outer coat, that makes them perfect for various climates. They are intelligent and can either be persistent or a snob depending on how they see you as a master. Treat them with respect but make sure that you also show them who is boss or they will decide that they are the boss in the house.

The Shiba Inu has an average life span of 12 to 15 years (the oldest I've heard of was a Shiba that lived to be 26) and is not prone to a lot of health problems except for slipped kneecaps and hip dysplasia. This is a bit unusual since those health problems are usually associated with larger breeds like Rottweilers. Males can grow up to 14 to 16 inches in height while the females can be 13 to 15 inches high. On average males weigh around 18 to 25 pounds and females weigh 15 to 20 pounds. Their double coat gives them great waterproofing, and cleanliness is not a big issue since they are a lot like cats when it comes to grooming themselves constantly. They do have some seasonal heavy shedding, usually in the spring although some shed once, twice, or even three times a year.

Chapter 2: A Dream or a Devil?

A Shiba Inu has such polar possibilities that it can either be your perfect dog or the dog from hell. Don't let the small size of this dog breed fool you, they can run all over the house and start biting and chewing on everything from the curtains and pillow to your hands. They do not bite to actually draw blood, although sometimes they do. Instead, they're really just exploring different objects with their mouth, which can be called mouthing. I actually call this "sharking," though I admit the term is completely made up.

So, let's talk about the pros and cons of a Shiba Inu.

The Dream Dog Perspective

It is a conveniently-sized dog with a strength that far exceeds its size. If you want to let your Shiba Inu off the leash in an enclosed park to allow him to play and run around, make sure that there are not a lot of small dogs or even dogs that are the same size as yours. When playing with other dogs, the Shiba Inu's match is closer to a Rottweiler than a Japanese Spitz. Remember, despite its adorable appearance, it is not a lap dog and was originally bred for hunting. Let's face it, if a dog can help you take down something as dangerous as an angry boar or bear, and is a few inches larger than a Japanese Spitz, it's too strong to be playing with small dogs.

Not only are they some of the strongest dogs around, they are also some of the best looking. They have a double coat with a fox-looking face and cinnabon-curled tail that looks a bit like a cinnabon. Some people like having dogs for protection, some want dogs to play with, and others simply like to have a good looking pet. With the Shiba Inu, you get all of these features wrapped up in one super-cute little package. They have what looks like an eternal smile and a very friendly face. Shiba Inus as a breed don't have a lot of variety when it comes to looks, so you will have a good idea about what to expect as far as how they will look when they grow up. Really the options only include color, as they come in foxy-reddish-orange, black, or white.

Shiba Inus are great playmates. They have a lot of energy and are definitely not lazy dogs. If you are into jogging, running, and even cycling, the Shiba Inu can be your best pal. It will be your perfect outdoor companion, by your side every step of the way. If you see yourself as an active sportsman or even a weekend warrior, the Shiba Inu could be your perfect dream dog.

The Shiba Inu is not only energetic but also light-footed, almost like a sneaky cat. So even if they run around the yard or even the house, they will most likely not disturb your afternoon nap unless they jump on you. They pack a lot of punch for a small package but they are also like a ninja when it comes to stealth. A quick browse on the internet and you can find loads of Shiba Inus running around without making a lot of noise.

The Bad Boy Perspective

As a result of their high energy, Shiba Inus need to be exercised regularly. If you don't take them for walks or runs very often, they will have to burn all of that energy somehow. They may do this by running all around the house, which can be a big problem if you have fragile belongings. They also like biting down on towels, pillows, socks, shoes, and underwear, so if you have a lot precious possessions, the Shiba Inu could be your worst nightmare.

Shiba Inus are also very suspicious of strangers or anybody they haven't spent a lot of time with in the past. This makes them good guard dogs, but if they are not properly socialized, they tend to be on the aggressive side with both animals and people even when you don't want them to. Many dogs are naturally great with kids but the Shiba Inu is not one of them. They don't like strangers and they typically don't like children. They also do not like other dogs around unless they grew up with them, especially when there's food in the picture. They like rough play too, and with their strength, their play might be too much for smaller dogs. If you want to have other dogs too, it's best to have a well-balanced and calm, larger breed dog like a Rottweiler or even a Pitbull.

It's a big challenge to keep them enclosed. They are very creative and clever when it comes to escaping and they also have strong tendencies to chase small animals. This also means they are not the best dogs to walk off a leash because if they see or smell something that catches their attention, they will run away with no regard to you standing there trying to call them back. In a well-secured yard is really the only place you should let them roam around freely. Keep in mind they can also jump relatively high so a three-foot fence might not be enough to stop them.

Shibas require a calm and assertive owner who has complete control of his or her own emotions, someone who will not simply shout the same command thinking that a louder volume will help. They also require a bit of maintenance due to their double coat and tendency to blow their undercoat twice a year. When this happens the amount of fur can be a bit shocking and even alarming for inexperienced dog owners. You will end up brushing out enough fur in volume to create a new dog almost.

The Shiba Inu is definitely a dog that you need a lot of patience and stamina for but they are not all bad. There is a reason why they were the chosen dog for the Japanese in the early days. The Shiba Inu are loyal, intelligent, and strong willed, often mirroring the characteristics of the Samurai. They are not the easiest to train but you would be surprised how well they will react to you if they sense that you are confident and sincere.

Chapter 3: What to Keep In Mind When Raising a Shiba

Shiba Inus were bred to be hunters. Unlike most modern day dogs, they do not have a lot of lazy tendencies. They are not lap dogs like Shih Tzu's or Pugs. They may not be as strong as a Rottie or a Pitbull but they can definitely be a handful when not properly socialized or trained. Shiba Inus are great companions and those who have been able to successfully train their Shiba can attest to all of their wonderful quirks. They are very intelligent, which means they can be very easy to train or can test your patience if they simply aren't in the mood to obey you. If you are someone who expects a dog that will roll over easily, or worse, think you are someone who can easily train a Shiba Inu with no experience or research, you should think again.

Don't Expect a Miracle

The first thing you need to know about Shiba Inus is that, despite their bad rap, they are like they are for a reason. They are primarily hunters and thus have the energy level and intelligence of a real hunting machine. Can they be trained? Yes. Can it be done in a week? Not even close. They are very intelligent, but their mental aptitude does not always mean they can be easily trained. In fact, lookout for your Shiba trying to actually outsmart you – which does happen from time to time. The Shiba's intelligence was originally used for hunting, not to "sit," "shake," or "play dead." This is a hunter and a skilled one at that. It takes the right attitude and patience to train a Shiba. It takes hours and hours of socializing, bonding, and training to ensure your Shiba will be a good companion. Even then, don't expect yours to turn out like Lassie.

If you can find humor in their clever antics, then a Shiba Inu is a great household companion. But having them in your house will require quite a lot of obedience training. Always remember to be calm and assertive but always be fair. Remember, they are not dumb animals. I'm not saying that they will be solving your kid's math homework any time soon but they can definitely tell if they have a calm and fair master or just an "I'm always right" kind of guy. Again, the Shiba Inu can have the tendency to bite things, including your hands, and sprint in circles around the house. Proper handling and exercise can definitely help, and it is important to remember not to raise your voice at them because they will not respond the way a Labrador would.

Do Not Be a Brute

Shiba Inus are not large dogs but they do have a lot of tendencies that might make them hard to control. One example of this is what is known to Shiba owners as the

Shiba 500. We will talk about that in detail later. Shiba Inus are sometimes described as much like a cat. They get bored easily and tend to do things at their own pace, but they also like being close to their master, though not within arm's reach. Remember that they were originally bred to hunt alongside humans so they really love being with people. The breed was never handled with force, but rather with relatively silent and somewhat intense mind games. They are not big dogs but do not let their size fool you. You should never, under any circumstances, try to man-handle your Shiba. Using force against your shiba will break his trust in your. On the other hand, you can't back down or else he'll think he's in charge.

The best way to manage your Shiba Inu is through what trainers often refer to as passive resistance. You can try this out by practicing taking your Shiba Inu on a walk when you want to rather than when he wants to. At first, of course, he will reject the idea and even ignore you. Do not tug on the leash because that will not work. If it looks like he does not want to follow you, let the idea go and go on with your normal activities. The next time your Shiba decides that it's time to go for a walk, he will try to catch your attention by whining or what is commonly known as the Shiba scream. The trick is to ignore him and, as time goes by, he will realize that he is not the one in charge and will then agree to follow your timetable. This does not require you to be physical. Instead, when they obey and do what you want, make sure to reward them with treats, kind words in a friendly tone, or a body massage.

Establish the Rules

Shiba Inus require structure in their lives and having rules and setting boundaries is necessary. You have to establish these rules, such as no biting, no aggression towards other animals, and no rough play, early on and you'll have to keep reinforcing them. All of these are known to be problems with the Shiba Inu. Establishing rules early on helps in minimizing bad behavior, if not completely eliminating it altogether.

1) No Sharking. Shiba Inus have a large tendency to bite (or "shark" as I call it) and according to various dog trainers who have successfully trained Shiba Inus, curbing this behavior can be done by simply imprinting to your dog that it is not an accepted behavior. Apply a mind game type of punishment like those you would give to a toddler like a time out or something like that, or stopping play and ignoring her for a while.

2) Possessiveness is Not Tolerated. Shiba Inus are like toddlers in many ways. Like a lot of kids, Shiba Inus are quite possessive of their toys and food, and do not like other dogs eating alongside them. They like their space and tend to react negatively when a lot of humans or other dogs are around. They easily feel cornered when this happens, especially when they are eating. To curb their possessiveness, use a series of reward training techniques that teach your Shiba it is okay to share.

3) Don't Play Too Roughly. Do not play any kind of rough games like wrestling or domination-oriented games like tug of war. If your Shiba has been socialized enough when it was young, wrestling with other dogs is quite alright, but do not engage in any type of domination game with your Shiba. This can cause them to become very competitive and play tug of war even when you are just walking them with a leash. Shiba Inus have a lot of energy so try playing other games with them, like fetch, ideally within your secure yard. That way, you get to spend quality time with your Shiba Inu while burning off some of their energy.

Socialize Your Shiba Inu

The Shiba Inu is a dog that loves to play rough and should only be let loose in a secure dog park if you know they have been well socialized with other dogs. The Shiba Inu loves to play and play hard. They tend to play rough, which may be too much for small or medium-sized dogs, but is just fine for larger dogs like Pitbulls or Rottweilers. Make sure that your Shiba's playmates are well socialized too or you might have fight on your hands and a fight between a Shiba Inu and a Rottweiler might not go well for your fury baby. He might look like a small fox, but he won't back down. You can start socializing your Shiba Inu through grooming and touching her while giving her treats, which helps to associate light physical contact with something positive.

Do not man-handle your Shiba Inu because it will fight you every step of the way. Keep your grooming positive by providing treats afterwards. If you try to handle your Shiba the wrong way, they will associate grooming with negativity and you don't want that. The Japanese did not pet the Shiba while reaching from above too often because they have a tendency to react negatively to it. It suggests dominance, which the Shiba Inu does not respond too well to. Considering that they are smaller dogs, this might be too hard to avoid, so instead make petting from above feel positive by providing treats or kind words in a friendly tone when doing so.

Manage Your Own Feelings

You know the saying "they can smell your fear"? Well, dogs can sense your energy and being negative about situations, like being afraid or nervous, gives them the feeling that they are the boss, which is not something that you want. You need to stay calm, not just on the outside but also in the inside. The tone of your voice and your body language will give your Shiba Inu the direction and command that it needs to follow you and not run all over you. Being naturally stubborn and self-confident, Shiba Inus require an equally well balanced and self-confident master, if not more so. It actually isn't that hard to do, simply stay calm and don't let your frustrations take over, and you'll be more than halfway to making your Shiba Inu a more obedient companion.

Once you get that ball of energy settled, you will have a dog with a great personality. They don't have a lot of health issues and when properly socialized, they can be your best pal which makes all of the worries and the training worth it. They can be great family pets and love children if they get to know them. Just make sure that the kids do not do any of the things that we cautioned you against earlier.

Training your Shiba Inu is a process you have to take one day at a time. Remember to be patient and not force the issue. Do not expect a miracle because your Shiba will not always care about your timeline or schedule. Do not try to force her to do what you want because it will be a long hard road if you do. Trying to force them will make them competitive and you do not want to go up against a Shiba. Establish the hierarchy early on and set rules for her to follow. Do it properly and she will understand what you want.

Chapter 4: Training Your Shiba Inu

At this point, you are well aware that a Shiba Inu is not for the first time dog owner and they can definitely test your patience. But they are very intelligent dogs which mean they have the capability of being trained for a number of obedience tricks like stay, heel, come, etc. It just seems that they are very hard to train for some people. But a seasoned trainer will trace the problem to the owner and not the dog itself. If the owner is impatient or doesn't know how to follow his own rule, then he is teaching his Shiba Inu that rules are meant to be broken and if you expect your intelligent dog to always follow your command, this is the worst thing that you can do.

Before we get into the individual commands, we need to establish the basic rules of teaching your Shiba Inu to do anything. The Shiba Inu is very intelligent and head-strong. It was specifically bred for hunting so you know that it is not a push-over. It has what others might refer to as an analytical brain. Some say that this is a bit of a stretch for a dog, but considering that they have shown the capacity to basically gauge their owner, it might very well be true. Just like how a hunter would analyze and learn the characteristics of his prey, the Shiba Inu also learns the personal traits of her owner. So here are a few pointers to keep in mind before getting into the actual training of your Shiba Inu.

Patience is a virtue

This is a basic requirement for dog training and is especially useful for Shiba Inus because they tend to test your patience a lot more than other breeds. For one, they are very intelligent and will tend to gauge you and the tone and energy of your voice to decide whether or not she actually has to obey. So figuring out the best tone of voice that your Shiba responds to is one thing that will require a lot of patience. If you do not have a lot of time and patience, then you should seriously re-think having such an intelligent breed as the Shiba Inu for a dog in the first place.

Always use your pet's name

Use your pet's name when you are training him to increase the attention that he gives you when you are calling him or giving him a command. This ensures that your Shiba Inu knows that you are talking to him and not somebody else. As a breed that is known to go on active hunts and not just a retriever, Shiba Inus are known to have tunnel vision when it sees something that can be a prey. Remember that Shiba Inus are naturally reserved and will tend to ignore their master from time to time so calling their name reinforces the idea that you are talking to him and he will actually pay attention.

Calling him by name also improves your relationship with your Shiba Inu reinforcing the idea that you are his master.

Reinforce a desired behavior

When your Shiba Inu does what you want him to do, always make sure that you reward him. It does not always have to be through food. Shiba Inus are keen in getting approval and a short massage on the chin or verbal approval like "Good boy" is enough to show him that you like what he just did.

Never reinforce undesired behavior

Shiba Inus are also very mischievous and will test your patience often. If you give in to their "cuteness" and head tilting, then you are encouraging him to do whatever he wants and simply win you over with those cute puppy-dog eyes whenever he sees that you are upset. Ignore him for a few minutes if he does not do what you want, and only reward him when he does exactly what you ordered him to do. Eventually, he will understand what you like and will do it again since they have a natural desire to please you.

Keep them interested

Always keep in mind that your Shiba Inu's attention is there only as long he is having fun. If he is not into what you are doing, he will just look away and look for something that he likes doing instead. So this means you should know when to quit while you're ahead. Do not squeeze in too many commands in one training session. One command at a time usually works best, and stop working on its repetitions when you see your Shiba losing interest. You can always pick it up again in an hour, or the next day.

So, now that you know the basics, let's start with the some of the most common commands that people like teaching their dogs. These commands are also very useful for more advanced commands and thus will act as the foundation for obedience or agility tasks that tend to work well for Shiba Inus.

LOOK

This command is very important in a sense that it makes your Shiba pay attention to you and nothing else. They have very short attention spans so having this command at your disposal allows you to teach him more commands later on. Being a natural hunting breed, they scan the surroundings a lot and get easily distracted by moving objects or animals like a cat or a mouse. Successfully teaching him to pay attention to you will come in handy later on, trust me.

Start by holding a treat in front of your face, right around the middle of your eyes then tell your Shiba to "Look", and if he looks at you, then reward him by giving him the treat. But you may ask, well, he's not really looking at me, he's looking at the treat. Well, yes. This is why, after a few repetitions, then you'll start hiding the treat in your hand and don't show it to him. Give the command again, if he looks at your face or makes eye contact, reward him. It he looks at your hand, say "no, no. Look," or, you can just wait until he eventually makes eye contact with you out of confusion for why he isn't getting the treat. Eventually, he'll catch on that he gets the treat when he looks at your face. If you do it often enough, he will learn to associate the command "Look" to that specific action and reward. The good thing about Shiba Inus is that they are very smart so they will catch on pretty quickly. It's best to practice with treats for a while, but then test him every so often without treats too so that in real-life situations (when you might not have a treat on hand), it will still work. Soon enough, the command will simply become like "muscle memory" for your Shiba, and you won't need treats at all.

SIT

Once you have established the "Look" command, you can now teach your Shiba Inu to "Sit". With your Shiba looking at you, hold the treat right above his nose. He will inevitably move his head up, move the treat farther towards between his propped up ears. The further you get, the lower his back end gets trying to reach it. As he eventually arrives at the natural "Sit" position, give him either a verbal reward or the treat itself while he is in the position. If he turns around or start doing something else, do not give him the treat. Do not hold the treat too high though. It's fine for the treat to actually touch his nose as long as you do not let him have it. Give it to him only when he is in the desired position.

Some trainers will say that this is harder to do than simply pushing the backside down to teach him to sit. However, this is not the best way to do it since Shiba Inus can be prone to hip dysplasia and pushing his hip down can actually cause more issues. Also, pinching or pushing him in place will not yield the best result since your Shiba Inu will most likely rebel since they do not like being man-handled. Just let the treat and your patience do the work. Always reward him whenever he does it properly, and soon, he will understand what you want him to do when he hears the command.

STAY

Now that you got your Shiba Inu to sit, the next thing he needs to learn is to "stay". Shiba Inus were bred to follow their master while hunting so he naturally wants to be on the move when you move. It is a lot better to teach him to stay while in a seated position than him just standing still because he can get on the move a lot faster when standing still than when seated. The seated position is also quite comfortable for him as opposed to standing up.

You can start teaching him to stay by asking him to sit. When he sits, take a small step backwards and say "Stay". If he does not move, head back over towards him and give him a treat. If he stands up, don't give the treat, and start over again by making him sit. You can then eventually work him up to staying for a minute. But remember that it will take a lot of practice on his end and patience on yours. Extend his "Stay" by walking further away from him and/or taking longer to reward him. This way, he will stay seated as long as he does not get his treat. With this command, it is better to use food for reward than just vocal praise. This way, your Shiba will know that if he stays, he will get to eat something as soon as you come back.

COME

Now that your Shiba knows how to sit and stay there, you can proceed to asking him to come. This command is very

31

useful obviously when you want your Shiba to come to you. This is also the first step if you want to eventually walk your Shiba Inu off leash. Remember though that not many Shiba owners have managed to train their Shibas not to run away when off leash, so be careful and take baby steps to build trust. You'll certainly want to be sure they follow your "Come" command when in a safe fenced in area every single time before you test out going off leash in an unsecure area.

Just like every command, teaching your Shiba to come will take a lot of time and patience. Start by either asking your Shiba to sit then call him to come using his name followed by "come". Something like "Buster, COME" and make sure you maintain eye contact. If your Shiba Inu comes to you, then reward him. It is also useful to use food or treats when teaching him to come, but try to interchange treats with verbal or physical approval like a "Good boy!", a massage or a combination of the two. With patience, your Shiba Inu will associate the word with what you want, and being a breed that has an inherent desire to please his master, soon he will always come either running or walking depending on the distance between you.

A trick that I use for the "Come" command is to give my Shiba a more specific action to associate with the command. So I actually bend or squat down, and put my hand out, fingers pointing down and palm towards my dog when I say "Come," and the responding action I'm looking for is her to touch the tip of her nose to my palm. So in reality, she doesn't understand the come command in that she has to walk over towards me, but she simply thinks I want her nose in my palm. Obviously as a consequence, she has to walk over towards me in order to accomplish that objective and get her treat or praise. You can choose to use this trick also, as it may help make the training a bit easier.

Do not chase your Shiba if he happens to run away after you give the command. This only means that they do not know what the command means. Chasing him will tell him that "Come" means that you want to chase him. Also, do not use a forceful voice because that can cause him to be afraid of you and associate the command with something negative. Voice tone control is key here: you always want to sound a little upbeat and friendly when giving commands.

LEAVE IT

This command is used to tell your Shiba to leave something alone. This is especially useful if you like visiting friends with your Shiba and you don't want him to start playing with your friend's belongings. Or, if you take your shoes off in your house, and don't want to have to constantly put them away or up high on shelves for fear that she'll destroy them. Having this command in your Shiba's understanding is a great way to ensure that she behaves for your and her well-being. Since the Shiba Inu is a naturally curious breed, even more so than a lot of other dog breeds, this command will have o be practiced first in an environment where there are not a lot of distractions.

Enter the room and once your Shiba reaches for an object in the room that she's not allowed to have, call your Shiba with his name followed by "Leave It". Since this command is more of a reprimand than a request, it's okay to use a firm or stern tone of voice. If she leaves the object alone, you'll want to immediately change your tone of voice to being friendly and full of praise, and you may choose to also reward with a treat. Eventually work your Shiba into a larger room or a room with more distractions. Through time, she will realize what "Leave It" means. This command is especially useful in making sure that your Shiba does not put anything in their mouth that can potentially harm them, such as a plugged in electrical cable for example.

HEEL

The command "Heel" is basically so that your Shiba Inu will not walk ahead of you and will instead follow you by your side in line with your heel. This is the origin of the command, as a matter of fact. This is quite useful if you are working towards walking your dog off leash. You can practice the command using a small room where you and your Shiba can walk around. Using a leash makes it easier for you to guide your Shiba and know where he needs to be. Do not attempt to do any corrections or reprimand when he moves ahead or behind though. Instead, just reward him if he stays slightly behind your right or left heel.

Walk with a relaxed body and do not let your Shiba pull you. If he pulls you, stop and guide him to where you want him to be and start walking again. Give the command "Heel" and if he stays in place while walking for a second or two, reward him. Eventually work the time up before giving him a treat until he can stay on heel for a whole minute. This means that your Shiba have a very good potential of eventually walking off leash in the future. As always, it only requires patience and a lot of practice.

OFF

The command "Off" is similar to "No" or "Stop", although some people use it to mean "Down" if the Shiba is jumping on something or someone. It's your choice really; as with any command, you can pick the word of your choice and use it to mean whatever you'd like. The principles behind training for almost any command are very similar, as you may have noticed already. Just try to keep the commands down to one syllable, or two at most. In this case, let's use "off" when you want your Shiba Inu to stop doing what he is currently doing and eventually make him understand that what he is doing is not acceptable behavior. As always, you do not correct the behavior by punishment like hitting him. Instead, reward him when he stops the behavior and always make eye contact. The first step is to establish to your Shiba that you are the master. Otherwise, you might give the command and he will not care because you're not the "boss".

If your Shiba doesn't obey the command, the most "punishment" you should offer is clapping your hands together to create an obnoxious noise. Be sure to accompany this sound with the command too though, so that eventually the command itself will suffice and you won't need to clap. As soon as he stops what he's doing, be sure to stop clapping and immediately start praising with a kind friendly voice again.

Once you have established that you have the "Alpha role", you can then give the command alone, whichever you prefer, in a calm but assertive voice. Not angry, not shouting, but firm and assertive. Your Shiba Inu will then stop and look at you, at which point you'll reward him. After enough practice, your Shiba Inu will know what the command means and will also have a good memory of what specific activities should not be done, like chewing your shoes, or jumping on your guests. If you are trying to make him stop a specific thing like biting, make sure that you do not engage him with games that will encourage what you are trying to correct. An example is biting. If you want him to stop the habit of biting stuff, then you should also stop playing games like tug of war or excessive rough playing.

FETCH

Fetch is probably the most recognizable game for any dog owner. It can be done properly once your Shiba Inu has gotten used to commands like "come" and "stay". Teaching fetch should be broken down to smaller steps or commands to make it easier for you and your Shiba. The first thing you need to teach your dog is to grab the item (a toy or a ball). You will need 2 of the item that you are training your Shiba with. Throw one of the toys nearby but do not let your Shiba off the leash at first. This will enable you to have more control and only let your dog to take the toy after you say "Fetch". Call your Shiba back using the "come" command then let him drop the toy by offering a treat, and you can eventually work in the "Drop" command here too. If he drops it, give him the treat and reinforce it by some verbal reinforcements like "good boy..." or something like that. Gradually increase the distance that you throw the toy, which also increases the time that your Shiba will tend to hold the toy in his mouth.

If your Shiba doesn't want to drop the toy when he brings it back to you, even when you say "Drop", the best way to deal with this is just to wait patiently until he realizes that the game won't continue until he lets go of the toy. It may take a minute or two to figure this out, but eventually he'll want to keep playing and therefore will drop it. Similarly, if he drops the toy without a problem, but it's out of your reach, you don't have to move and go get it. Instead, just give him a couple minutes to figure out that the game can't continue until he brings it all the way to your hand. In the game of Fetch, you really don't need to use treats as a reward, since playing the game itself is reward enough for your Shiba.

If your Shiba seems distracted at all when first starting out with this command, you may need to move to a smaller space with fewer distractions, for example a small bedroom instead of the large yard.

Chapter 5: Grooming Your Shiba Inu

Shiba Inus usually keep themselves very well groomed, without much work you'll have to do. Their double coat is almost perfect, and a natural dirt repellant. Furthermore, they love to groom themselves like cats, constantly licking and cleaning all parts of their own bodies. Don't give them a bath too often because that can take away the waterproofing nature of their coats little by little. But do make sure that you brush their coat often to help deal with their shedding, especially when the weather changes and you start to notice heavier shedding or coat-blowing.

Shiba Inu Hygiene

When it comes to hygiene, Shiba Inus are a lot more like cats than dogs. They generally do not require your help in grooming because they tend to groom themselves. During these self-grooming sessions, they release natural oils that help them maintain their body temperature and keep their skin properly moisturized, as well as keeping their coat waterproof. Trying to give them a bath too often can actually be a negative for your Shiba Inu since that will remove the natural oil coating that their upper coat has. Taking away their natural oil coating can cause various health issues like unusual hair loss and itchiness. If your Shiba Inu gets too dirty to clean himself up, you can use a dampened cloth to scrub it off, but do not use shampoo frequently.

Blowing Their Coat

As previously mentioned, twice a year your Shiba Inu will go through periods of heavy shedding known to seasoned Shiba Inu owners and trainers as "blowing their coat." Shiba Inus have a very luscious undercoat that they usually shed in the spring. The undercoat works its way to the top coat and will look like soft patches of fur that's zig-zag shaped. Your Shiba will look rather funny during this time but you can simply pluck those patches off your fur baby without hurting them. Actually, they will rather appreciate it because they like feeling clean and groomed. Regularly brushing their coat during this season of heavy shedding will help a lot in keeping things neat and tidy, not just on your Shiba's coat but in your house as well. As a matter of fact, by the time he is done blowing his coat, you may have collected enough undercoat to make a large bed pillow. For first time Shiba Inu owners, it might even be hard to believe that this is normal and people often bring their dogs to the vet thinking that their Shiba Inu might have some kind of allergy or skin disease.

Proper Grooming

Blowing their coat usually takes about two to three weeks. You will need to brush their coat more than once a day but when they are done with this period they will go back to their normal, minimal, shedding routine. While this period might be quite surprising and worrying for you, shedding does not hurt your Shiba Inu and they actually will let you brush them as much as you can, as long as you don't do it too roughly. You taking away their blown coat actually makes them trust you more and the physical contact gives you a chance to show your Shiba Inu that your touch can be a loving and positive thing. Once they associate your touch with something positive, you will be able to pet him a lot more, as will other members of your family. This can be a great opportunity for you to spend some quality time with your Shiba Inu, which can make the difference in your effort to have a well-balanced and socialized dog.

Off Season Shedding

Shiba Inus shed during spring to lose the thick undercoat that they had to help them maintain their temperature in the winter. Normally this shedding happens once or twice a year but there are those who shed heavily three times a year. The key is to observe your Shiba closely and if they are shedding heavily at a time that is outside the normal shedding pattern that has been established in the past, then that is off season shedding. If your Shiba Inu is shedding for extended amounts of time or off season, then you may need to look into it, as another cause for off season shedding is parasites. Shiba Inus are especially vulnerable to certain kinds of flea infections. A flea infection can be quite hard to detect since Shiba Inus have quite a thick coat, but regular brushing should allow you the chance to keep a close eye on your Shiba Inu's skin health status. Generally speaking, as a good practice, I try to take a look through my Shiba's fur for a few minutes for fleas and ticks every few days or at least once a week, even though I only find something once or twice a year. If you notice your Shiba scratching herself more than normal, you may want to do a more thorough inspection to see if any fleas are in there and up to no good.

If your Shiba Inu is shedding abnormally off season, then you might want to look into the possibility that they have internal health issues. If you are not a seasoned Shiba Inu owner, you should definitely consult a vet because the faster that your Shiba Inu's health problem gets diagnosed, the quicker it can be treated. It can be as small as an allergic reaction to something in the environment like pollen or an ingredient in their food, or it could be something as serious as some kind of gland or organ dysfunction. Either way, the sooner that it is identified, the better off your Shiba will be.

Chapter 6: The Shiba Inu's Health Profile

The Shiba Inu is a fairly healthy breed, but it does have a genetic pre-disposition to a few diseases and health concerns. Obviously not all Shiba Inus will have the same health problems, but their general level of activity does make them most prone to certain issues that can be addressed if properly diagnosed in the early stages.

Hip Dysplasia

This is a bit of a head-scratcher in a small and sturdy breed like the Shiba Inu. Hip dysplasia is more commonly seen in larger breeds, but it has been observed that more and more Shiba Inus are developing this problem. Shiba Inus have very compact and muscular bodies, but they actually don't have the strongest bones. This is thought to be why some develop hip dysplasia in their later years in life.

Patellar Luxation (Knee Cap Displacement)

This is the displacement of the knee cap, and ranges from grade one, where the patella is displaced but can return to normal, to grade four, where the patella is luxated all the time and often requires corrective surgery. It can be hard to notice this on your pup since we are used to seeing them struggle with walking, but the problem can actually be diagnosed as early as the first five weeks of a young puppy's life.

Cataracts

Cataracts are a health problem that almost all smaller dogs seem to share. Juvenile cataracts, as they are called to distinguish it from the normal clouding of the eye on older dogs, are potentially blinding. Not to worry, the diagnosis and treatment of juvenile cataracts is pretty accurate and there's not a lot of risk involved.

Obviously, these are not the only health problems that your Shiba Inu may experience, but according to the National Shiba Club of America, most health problems reported for the breed are isolated issues rather than proven hereditary and breed specific concerns. Organizations like the Canine Health Information Center, the Orthopedic Foundation for Animals, and the Canine Eye Registration Foundation all agree that a Shiba Inu has a fairly good chance of staying healthy as long as they get regularly checked by a licensed vet. As with all things medical, prevention is always better than treatment.

Chapter 7: The Shiba Inu's Quirks

The typical Shiba Inu has a lot of quirks such that, if you aren't patient, you might give up in just a few days. Not all Shiba Inus are the same, but just like every breed of dog, they do have inherent tendencies specific to their breed. These tendencies have their own pros and cons. What we will be talking about in this chapter are the common quirks you can expect from your Shiba Inu and how you can deal with them. Just remember, there is not one quick trick when it comes to turning Shiba Inus into model citizens.

The Shiba 500

It sounds like a long range race like that run by Siberian Huskies known as the Iditarod, doesn't it? To understand what the Shiba 500 is, you have to trace back years and years into the breed's history and by now, you are well aware that they were bred to be hunting dogs. They took an active part in hunting trips, and weren't there to merely retrieve the game after it had been killed. They know how to use their speed and strength, and yes they are very strong for their size. What comes from their natural predatory instinct is, in a more domestic setting, often referred to by Owners as the Shiba 500, and here's how it goes:

51

The Shiba Inu tends to run around the house like a crazy animal for a good five minutes, for some even more, and for no apparent reason. She will choose an arbitrary "track," whether it be a simple circle, a figure 8, or a more complex course including jumps, tunnels, or other obstacles. If you happen to be in the room during the Shiba 500, you may find yourself becoming one of the course obstacles in face. Sometimes the Shiba 500 even involves a good amount of biting or growling, and she may choose a random object in the room and treat it like a temporary sparring enemy. If you have a good sense of humor, you will probably find the Shiba 500 pretty entertaining, even hilarious at times.

But is this behavior really breed specific? If you look at various dog breeds, you will notice that a lot of them share this excessive amount of energy. Dog breeds from Pitbulls all the way to Shih Tzu's have a form of behavior that is similar to this. Although, most will not include biting, this is not unheard of for Shiba Inus. Some would ask the question, if Shiba Inus' bloodline isn't directly connected to that of wolves, why does it have so many predatory instincts?

Shih Tzu's are by far the closest relative of the wolf when it comes to modern dog breeds so why does the Shiba Inu have so much more of a tendency to bite during these manic phases than a Shih Tzu? Well, because the difference between Shiba Inus and Shih Tzu's is that Shih Tzu's are bred specifically to be lapdogs. They were not intended to hunt while the Shiba Inu was breed specifically for that purpose.

They needed to have this predatory trait at their disposal when they were hunting because you cannot kill a wild boar with cuteness and long flowing hair. Shiba Inus had to be smart, agile, and strong, which they are. Since these predatory urges are no longer being utilized today, modern Shiba Inus have to burn off the energy that used to be utilized during a hunt, hence, the excessive running and occasional biting.

However, if you get your Shiba Inu regular exercise and have had him on a proper routine since he was a puppy, there is a great chance of curbing this tendency. You might not be able to completely take it away yet but you are off to a great start. At the end of the day, it boils down to energy and the Shiba Inu has a lot of it. It's like you having a quadruple shot of expresso. You get a jolt of energy all of a sudden and you have to do something to burn it off. Well, the Shiba Inu has that hardwired in his system to kick in at various times of the day. If you are lucky enough to have a Shiba Inu that has fairly "scheduled" occasions of the Shiba 500, you can try and do a pre-emptive strike or a preventive measure by taking them on an hour walk before they get this urge to run around. This way, they will be pretty much spent and no longer feel the need to "chase" their imaginary prey all around the house.

Alternatively, you can just sit back, watch, be entertained, enjoy, and even play along.

The Shiba Scream

Shiba Inus rarely bark. If they do bark at something, it is usually worth looking into. But if you try to force your Shiba Inu to do something they don't want to do (like take a bath) or restrict them from food, then you will most likely be treated to what is known to Shiba owners as the Shiba Scream. This is when they make a sound that is entirely unique to the Shiba Inu. A lot of dogs whine when they want something but no dog can whine quite like the Shiba Inu. It sounds a lot like a small child throwing a screaming and crying fit, which is why a lot of Shiba Inu owners have had visits from their neighbors, or concerned citizens and even in some cases, the police called by a neighbor who said that they heard a cry or a scream of a baby. If you want to know more about the Shiba Scream, just do a quick internet search for the endless videos Shiba owners have posted in places like Youtube. One thing is for sure, if your Shiba Inu is screaming, he wants something specific, and he definitely wants you to pay attention. If you get a chance to actually have a Shiba Inu and hear this infamous scream, you will never forget it.

Miscellaneous

Just like all dog breeds, no Shiba Inu is exactly the same as another. Some like going out in the yard to play around in the spring time while others like playing in the rain. One of the more common Shiba Inu quirks though, is that they can be sociable with other types of male dogs but can be quite dominant when there are other male Shibas in the area, or worse, in the household.

When it comes to petting your Shiba, make sure you do it by giving a light massage under the neck or chin, and approaching him from within his field of vision with your hand down low. Being pet from above triggers a natural reaction of being attacked, and your Shiba will display natural defensiveness. They are small dogs so when they get attacked, it is usually from above. If you want to be friends with a Shiba Inu and earn their trust, approach them properly, at least until you've established a bond of total trust which may take up to several years.

Chapter 8: The Shiba as a National Treasure

In an earthquake that hit Japan in 2004, a Shiba Inu actually sought out and led rescuers to the damaged home of his owners, leading to the rescue of an elderly man and a young girl. This was then made into a movie (Mari and the three puppies) which further improved the reputation of the breed as one of the most loyal and intelligent dogs in the world. The Shiba Inu is very tenacious and fiercely protective of his human pack. He was not just a hunting companion, he was also a valued part of a Japanese family in the old days up until today. As a matter of fact, the Shiba Inu was declared a national treasure of Japan in 1936 which further solidified their status as the most popular companion dog in the Land of the Rising Sun. In 2008, a Shiba Inu named Kika was showed online and had a live "puppy-cam" which was streamed over the internet and was one of the biggest and most popular live streams, attracting millions of hits. Lately, there has been a video uploaded and is making the rounds, of a Shiba Inu watching over a store, seemingly able to "converse" with customers.

Disobedient yet Devoted

Shiba Inus are not always up for restraints like wearing a collar. It can take months and even years to properly train them to walk on a leash. They are quite smart too and can run away if they ever figure out how to slip through their collar, which is why death by car accident is one of the leading causes of death for the breed. They have a great sense of direction which is why they never get lost but the modern obstacle known as vehicle traffic is something they haven't figured out yet. They can be one of the most devoted family pets a person could hope for. They do not really become destructive around the house when you leave them behind, but they do have ways of making you feel guilty. It could be the lonely stare that they give you as you're walking out the door, or the fact that they get really sad when watching you go, but on the flip side, the tail-wagging and excited greeting that you'll receive upon arriving back at home is priceless.

Sociable but Aloof

A Shiba Inu will never be happy living in a dog pound, or even visiting one. They are at their best when around people they trust and have come to love. Even so, if you simply give them a command, chances are they will not respond if they don't see any reason to follow it. They have a mind of their own, and they need to trust you first and this is why when there are strangers in the house, you will not see your Shiba Inu welcoming them or even allowing them to touch him. He will most likely not even be in the same room. But if they see the guest often enough, they can be very sweet towards them.

When it comes to children, Shiba Inus are somewhat of a wild card. Remember that in Japan, kids are not as playful as the children are in the US nowadays. Children today will flock around a dog to try and touch him and pet him. This might be too much for a Shiba Inu and might make him feel cornered. As with most animals, the Shiba will also put up their guard when cornered. If you want to have a Shiba Inu in your house and you have children, teach your children to approach the Shiba one at a time, and to avoid petting on the head or tail, at least at first until he realizes that you mean no harm to him and thus will treat you as part of his human pack. Trust is something that you will have to work for with a Shiba Inu.

Note: There are of course the rare cases of Shibas that absolutely love human interaction. My Shiba, in fact, glances at most strangers trying to make eye contact and receive their attention and adoration, and when she gets it, she puts on her cutest act and greets everyone with tail-wagging excitement. All the other Shiba owners that I've met, however, agree that this is very rare behavior for a Shiba. Oddly enough though, I believe she can recognize when a person has bad intentions, as she typically offers a single bark or disapproving grumble when the antagonist appears in a movie.

Can Read Emotions

You can be a Golden Globe winning actor but you cannot fool a Shiba Inu with a fake smile. He will see through all the B.S. and somehow know what you are really up to. This is one of the reasons why the Japanese revered the Shiba Inu: because it can almost detect if someone has honor or not. This is why they are also great guard dogs because even if a thief offers him food, he will often ignore the food and keep a suspicious eye on the thief. Unlike most dogs that will bark a lot whenever there is someone in front of the house who might not readily be a threat, a Shiba Inu will try and gauge what you are up to. They have a great capacity for judging if someone is a threat or not.

They can even feel many things that, at least for some, suggest that they can tell if there is an impending calamity. Many animals are believed to have this ability and Shiba Inus have been seen barking like crazy and being unusually tenacious in getting their master's attention prior to a major natural disaster like an earthquake or flood.

Fearful but Courageous

This might sound contradictory but that is exactly what a Shiba Inu is sometimes. They can be afraid of many things like traffic, planes, or trains. You will have to put in the time to earn their trust but once you do have it, they will be there to protect you at all costs. They are ready to fight off any perceived threat to their master and are known to fight to the death if necessary. They seem to be impervious to pain when in full attack mode, a possible remnant of their hardcore hunting lineage, and this means that you can trust them with your life once they see you as their master. Much like the famed Samurai, they will not think twice before defending their territory or family.

Not Just a Dog

Anybody who has handled a Shiba Inu will tell you that they are a handful and they most definitely are. By this alone, you can safely assume that they are not your regular type of dog. They cannot simply be called just a dog. Shiba Inus are some of the most intelligent and unique animals that one can ever have, especially as a domesticated friend. Great respect and contentment comes with having a Shiba Inu by your side. You do not only end up with a loyal and loving companion, you also develop a connection to nature and a further understanding of how things ought to be. This might be hard for some to comprehend but anybody who has successfully socialized their Shiba Inu will agree. After all, you don't become a national treasure by barking and looking cute, right?

Chapter 9: The Future for the Breed

The Shiba Inu breed has a bright future ahead of it. It is one of a few domesticated animals that was declared a national treasure and that alone ensures the breed's existence for the foreseeable future. But what really makes the Shiba Inu such a good breed to bet on is that it is not your typical dog. Unlike toy dogs and extremely large dogs, the Shiba Inu has a great set of characteristics that will never go out of style. The future of the breed is not just in the hands of the breeders. It is in the hands of each and every one of the Shiba Inu owners all around the world. Remember that they were almost completely wiped out in World War II but the resilient breed was able to bounce right back and, though they no longer need to serve the primary purpose of hunting that they were bred for, they have such a great following that Shiba Inu owners alone can ensure that the breed will continue to flourish.

For a lot of dog breeds, the future of the breed itself depends heavily on the integrity of the handful of breeders but the Shiba Inu has a strong enough following that even regular owners who happen to have a couple can have their dogs breed and produce purebred Shiba Inus. The Shiba Inu has a very distinct look that you can readily recognize when you see it; it isn't like a lot of the dog breeds that seem to be carbon copies of each other with very subtle differences. The breed is fairly healthy and has a relatively short list of hereditary health problems. You can look at a Shiba Inu as a great canvas where, if you mean well, you will undoubtedly end up with a masterpiece of a dog. However, keep in mind that if you do not put in the time and patience, you will have a dog that is not just hard to control but might very well bite you in the bum in the near future.

A Shiba Inu is also like a Pitbull in a sense that even if they grew up with an abusive or undeserving owner, they can bounce back and be the best pal that you could ever hope for. There are a lot of places where one can rescue a Shiba Inu and once socialized properly, they can be the best house pet and you can even trust them around kids as long as they've become a familiar part of the family. All it takes is a confident and well-balanced owner and the Shiba Inu will be by your side for years and years to come.

Conclusion

Well, this just about covers everything you might possibly need to know about the Shiba Inu breed. I hope my love for these intelligent, entertaining, and adorable little creatures has shone through and maybe even rubbed off a little on you, unless you were a Shiba Lover already.

And last, I'd like to truly thank you for purchasing this book and taking time to read it all the way through! If you enjoyed it or found it helpful, I'd greatly appreciate it if you'd take a moment to leave a review on Amazon. Thank you!

Made in the USA
Monee, IL
06 January 2021